AF228584

# MILITARY SHIPS

Martha London

DiscoverRoo
An Imprint of Pop!
popbooksonline.com

abdobooks.com

Published by Pop!, a division of ABDO, PO Box 398166, Minneapolis, Minnesota 55439. Copyright © 2020 by POP, LLC. International copyrights reserved in all countries. No part of this book may be reproduced in any form without written permission from the publisher. Pop!™ is a trademark and logo of POP, LLC.

Printed in the United States of America, North Mankato, Minnesota.

052019
092019

THIS BOOK CONTAINS RECYCLED MATERIALS

Cover Photo: Shutterstock Images

Interior Photos: Shutterstock Images, 1; Alexei Pavlishak/TASS/Getty Images, 5; Evgeniy Maloletka/AP Images, 6; Alexey Malgavko/Sputnik/AP Images, 7; US Navy, 8–9, 21, 26; iStockphoto, 11, 14, 20, 24–25, 28 (top), 30, 31; Witold Krasowski/Alamy, 12; Pictures Colour Library/Travel Pictures/Alamy, 13; Brian_Kinney/Alamy, 15; The Picture Art Collection/Alamy, 17; US Naval History and Heritage Command, 18; US National Archives and Records Administration, 19, 29 (top), 29 (bottom); Defense Visual Information Distribution Service, 23, 27; Library of Congress, 28 (bottom)

Editor: Connor Stratton
Series Designer: Jake Slavik

Library of Congress Control Number: 2018964857

Publisher's Cataloging-in-Publication Data

Names: London, Martha, author.

Title: Military ships / by Martha London.

Description: Minneapolis, Minnesota : Pop!, 2020 | Series: Inside the military | Includes online resources and index.

Identifiers: ISBN 9781532163869 (lib. bdg.) | ISBN 9781644940594 (pbk.) | ISBN 9781532165306 (ebook)

Subjects: LCSH: Naval ships--Juvenile literature. | Warships--Juvenile literature. | Aircraft carriers--Juvenile literature. | Military vehicles--Juvenile literature.

Classification: DDC 359.83--dc23

# WELCOME TO DiscoverRoo!

Pop open this book and you'll find QR codes loaded with information, so you can learn even more!

Scan this code* and others like it while you read, or visit the website below to make this book pop!

popbooksonline.com/military-ships

*Scanning QR codes requires a web-enabled smart device with a QR code reader app and a camera.

# TABLE OF CONTENTS

# CHAPTER 1
# MILITARY SHIPS IN ACTION

The Sea of Azov lies between Ukraine and Russia. In 2015, Russia claimed that Ukraine needed permission to enter the sea. But in 2018, Ukraine's ships tried to enter anyway. Fighting broke out.

*Russia used ships to block the entrance to the Sea of Azov.*

Russia saw the Ukrainian ships as a threat. One Russian ship rammed into a Ukrainian ship. Russian sailors fired. Helicopters came to help. Six people were wounded. The Ukrainian ships were captured.

*Russian ships forced Ukrainian ships to dock at a nearby port.*

Military ships have a variety of uses. They can attack enemy ships. They can protect a country's coasts. They can also guard merchant ships.

*A US destroyer works with other ships to protect a merchant ship.*

**DID YOU KNOW?** Merchant ships carry goods to be sold. Military ships help make sure these goods reach their destinations.

# EARLY MILITARY SHIPS

People have used military ships since ancient times. Many early ships had **oars**. Sailors rowed to power the ships. Early ships stayed close to shore. These ships could not sail on the open sea.

A model of an ancient Greek warship sails close to shore.

Militaries built larger ships in the 1600s and 1700s. On these ships, tall **masts** held up large sails. Wind filled the sails and pushed the ships along. With the wind, ships could move farther from shore. But they moved slowly. They were also difficult to steer.

*During the 1700s, one common type of warship was known as a brig.*

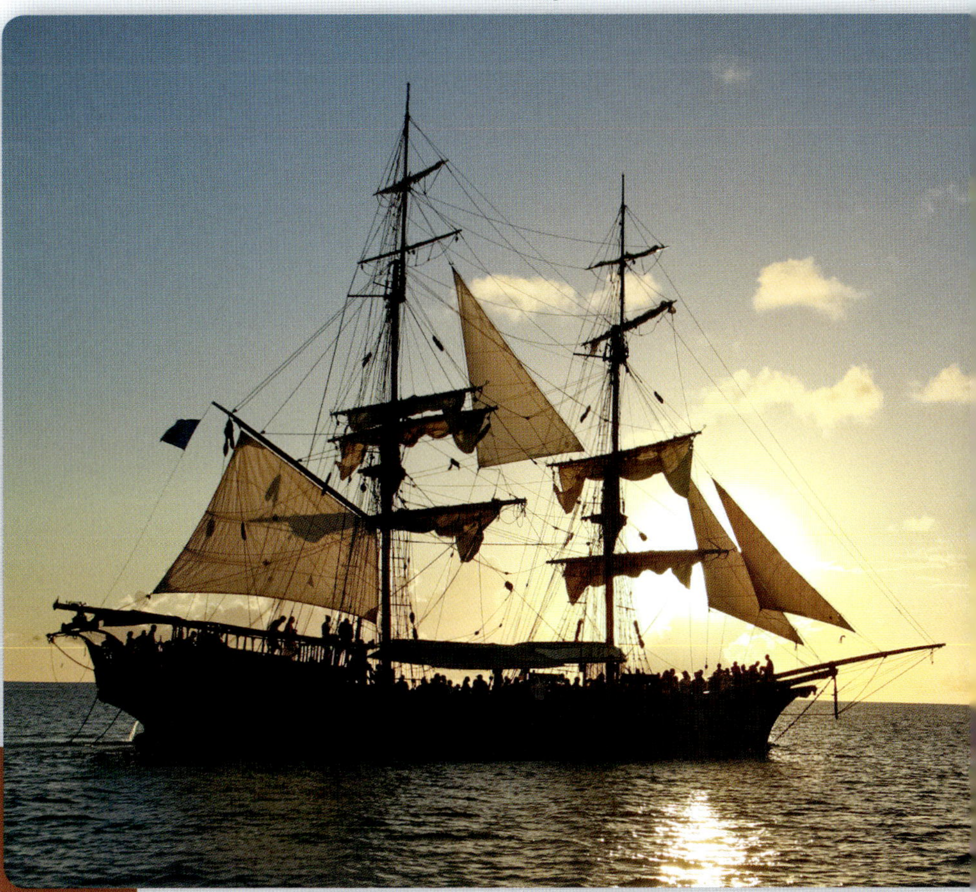

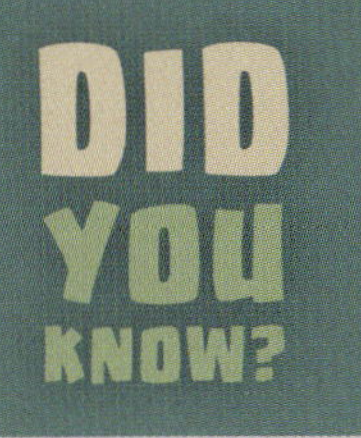

**DID YOU KNOW?**

**Wind-powered ships could not turn around until the wind changed direction.**

Many ships had cannons. Militaries fired cannonballs at enemy ships. Cannonballs could punch large holes in a ship's wooden side. These holes would cause the enemy ship to sink. Militaries fought naval battles this way for hundreds of years.

# PARTS OF A WARSHIP, 1700s

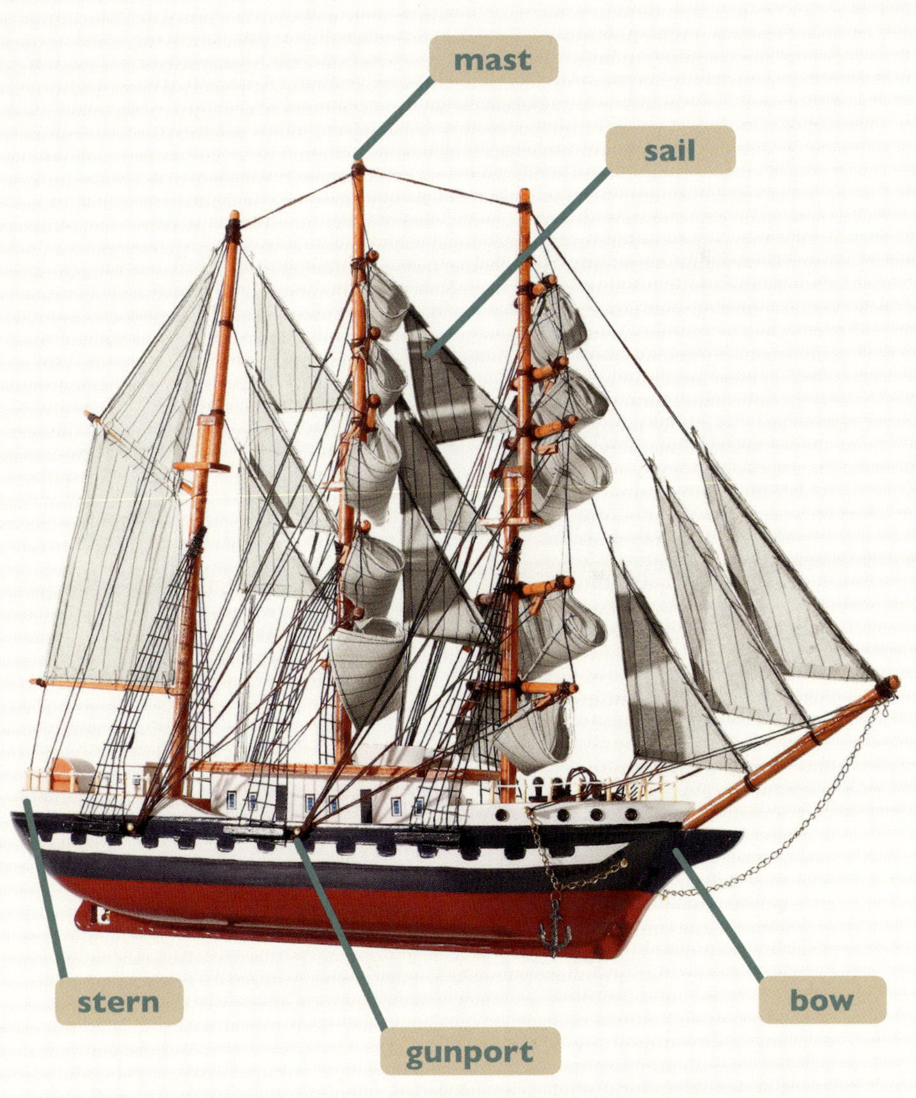

During the 1800s, several inventions changed how ships worked. Steam power made ships faster. The steam engines powered propellers under the water.

*The first US steam-powered warship was built in 1814.*

Propellers have metal plates that spin. Propellers and **rudders** made steering easier.

In the early 1860s, the US Navy built one of the first iron-covered military ships.

Builders began using metal in their ships. First, they covered ships with iron plates. These plates protected the

wooden ships. Then,

builders began making

ships of steel.

Today's military ships have moved
away from steam power. In the 1950s,
some ships began using **nuclear
power**. Other ships use gas engines.
The engines burn fuel to power
the propellers.

USS *New Jersey* set the record
for fastest battleship in 1968.
It had a top speed of nearly
41 miles per hour.

The US Navy built the first nuclear-powered aircraft carrier in 1961.

# CHAPTER 4
# MILITARY SHIPS TODAY

Battleships today come in many sizes.

Some battleships are narrow. They are

able to travel in shallow water. Other

battleships are huge. These ships travel

the ocean.

**DID YOU KNOW?**

Military ships go to sea for a few weeks each month for training. Longer trips might last for six to nine months.

Aircraft carriers are another type of military ship. Militaries first used these ships in World War II (1939–1945). Planes can take off from these ships.

*Aircraft carriers are massive. They must be able to carry a lot of equipment.*

The planes can return to the carrier after completing their missions. As a result, planes do not have to land in enemy countries.

Today's military ships use ECDIS to navigate. ECDIS is a computer system. It helps ships plan and monitor their routes. It uses GPS to track the ship's location. Militaries will continue to find new technologies to improve their ships.

*The US Navy uses computer systems to imitate the experience of sailing battleships. Students can train on these systems before sailing the actual ship.*

A US sailor uses a computer system to navigate a battleship.

# TIMELINE

## 1571

Ships with **oars** fight in a massive battle off the coast of Greece.

## 1815

The first steam-powered warship is built for the US Navy.

## 1862

Iron-plated ships first meet in battle during the US Civil War (1861–1865).

## 1880s

The US Navy starts building steel ships.

## 1963

GPS is created. It uses satellites to work.

## 1941

Aircraft carriers play a major role during World War II.

# MAKING CONNECTIONS

### TEXT-TO-SELF

What kind of military ship would you want to see up close? Why?

### TEXT-TO-TEXT

Have you read another book about a military vehicle? How is that vehicle's job similar to a military ship's job? How is it different?

### TEXT-TO-WORLD

Many inventions helped improve military ships. Which invention do you think improved ships the most?

# GLOSSARY

**GPS** – short for "Global Positioning System," a system that uses information from satellites to determine an object's location on Earth.

**mast** – a tall pole that holds up a ship's sails.

**navigate** – to plan and manage the course of a ship or other vehicle.

**nuclear power** – the process of splitting tiny particles to produce energy.

**oar** – a pole with a flat blade that sailors can use to move a boat through the water.

**rudder** – a flat piece of wood or metal located at the back of a ship and used for steering.

# INDEX

# ONLINE RESOURCES

# popbooksonline.com

Scan this code* and others like it while you read, or visit the website below to make this book pop!

## popbooksonline.com/military-ships

*Scanning QR codes requires a web-enabled smart device with a QR code reader app and a camera.